JANE WILKINSON LONG

JANE WILKINSON LONG
Texas Pioneer

By Neila Skinner Petrick

Illustrated by Joyce Haynes

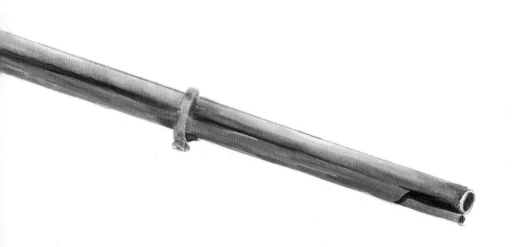

PELICAN PUBLISHING COMPANY
Gretna 2004

To all the children who love to read

*The word "Pelican" and the depiction of a pelican are trademarks
of Pelican Publishing Company, Inc., and are registered
in the U.S. Patent and Trademark Office.*

Library of Congress Cataloging-in-Publication Data

Petrick, Neila Skinner.
  Jane Wilkinson Long : Texas pioneer / by Neila Skinner Petrick ; illustrated by Joyce Haynes.
       p. cm.
Summary: An introduction to the life of Jane Wilkinson Long, a Texas pioneer who experienced the early days of that state and who was the mother of the first Anglo baby born there.
  ISBN 1-58980-147-4 (hardcover : alk. paper)
 1. Long, Jane Herbert Wilkinson, 1798-1880—Juvenile literature. 2. Women pioneers—Texas—Biography—Juvenile literature. 3. Pioneers—Texas—Biography—Juvenile literature. 4. Texas—Biography—Juvenile literature. 5. Frontier and pioneer life—Texas—Juvenile literature. [1. Long, Jane Herbert Wilkinson, 1798-1880. 2. Pioneers. 3. Women—Biography. 4. Texas—History—19th century.] I. Haynes, Joyce, ill II. Title.
  F389.L85 P48 2004
  976.4'04'092—dc22

                                                                2003018915

Printed in China
Published by Pelican Publishing Company, Inc.
1000 Burmaster Street, Gretna, Louisiana 70053

JANE WILKINSON LONG

Jane Wilkinson Long stood on the porch looking out at her family's plantation. Years before, Jane, an orphan, had come to live with her aunt and uncle in Natchez, Mississippi. On this summer's day in 1819, she would be leaving her home.

At sixteen, she had married Dr. James Long. He wanted to conquer a distant land called Texas, ruled by Spain. Spain also owned neighboring Mexico. He gathered an army and rode away. Now, at twenty, she would follow Dr. Long west. Jane put a bridle and saddle on her little gray mule, Agatha, and set out for faraway Texas.

To keep her safe, Dr. Long had sent soldiers to travel with her. Jane's daughter Ann and Kiamatia, a slave who had been with Jane since they were children, rode with them in a wagon over the rough countryside.

First, Jane hired a riverboat captain to ferry her group across the great Mississippi River. Once across the river, they rode to Alexandria, Louisiana, where Jane's sister Barbara Calvitt lived. They soon continued on to Texas.

One day, Jane and Agatha came to the Sabine River, which separated Louisiana and Texas. If Agatha wouldn't cross, Jane knew there was danger. Agatha looked both ways and plunged into the fast-flowing water. Jane held on tight!

Agatha scrambled up the far bank. Jane waved at her family and the soldiers across the river. They would join her soon.

Jane was in Texas! The word *Tejas*, derived from the Caddo Indians, meant friendship. She was eager to explore the new land. There were armadillos, gray wolves, coyotes, black bears, mountain lions, bison, and a strange horned toad. Deer grazed in the thick forest. Agatha trotted through tall pine, live oak, and hickory trees. Brightly colored birds flitted above—robins, blue jays, and cardinals.

Agatha's ears lay forward, flopping up and down as she trotted. That is how a mule carries its ears when it feels safe. Suddenly, one of Agatha's ears pointed straight ahead and the other straight back. That was a sure sign of danger.

Jane slipped off the mule onto the soft pine needles covering the ground. She listened without making a sound. Nearby, voices spoke an unfamiliar language. An Indian hunting party!

These Indians might be friendly, or they might not.
Jane crouched beside Agatha. Her heart pounded. In a
little while, the voices faded. Jane patted Agatha while
she waited for Ann and Kiamatia.

Something stirred in the
tall grass. Had the hunting
party come back? Agatha
stomped her hooves. A mule
could hurt its enemies with its sharp
hooves.

A small creature scurried past Jane. She held her nose.

A skunk! What a relief!
About that time, the others joined Jane. Together they continued their journey deeper into Texas.

Finally, Jane joined Dr. Long and his army in a fort at Point Bolivar near Galveston Island. The soldiers prepared for war. In 1821, Dr. Long and his army left to conquer Mexico, leaving Jane, Ann, and Kiamatia alone on the Bolivar Peninsula.

Jane searched for food. One day, she saw a dog
chasing a bear across the sandy beach. She called to
the dog and he came, wagging his tail. She named him
Galveston for the nearby island.

One day, Jane shot a duck for her hungry family to eat.
Galveston retrieved the bird and decided to keep it for
himself. But Jane convinced him to bring her the duck.

Jane was expecting a baby. On a cold winter's night in December of 1821, Mary James Long was born.

Then one afternoon, Kiamatia saw canoes coming toward the fort. Tall Indians with their faces painted red and black paddled very fast. They did not look friendly. They were fierce Karankawa Indians!

Outside the fort was a cannon. Next to the cannon was a bent flagpole. Jane raised a flag over the fort—a red flannel petticoat.

She found cannonballs, loaded the cannon, and fired at the canoes. A cannonball flew over the water and made a thunderous splash. The Indians thought soldiers were firing the cannon and they paddled away as fast as they could.

The Indians frightened Jane. It was time to leave! Soon after this incident, she received a message from Mexico City. Jane's husband, Dr. Long, had died mysteriously. Now, she alone was responsible for her family. Where would they go?

Jane learned that Stephen Austin was leading settlers into Texas. Stephen was an attorney, mapmaker, and farmer. He loved his Austin colony. The family could remain in the territory! Jane joined Austin's colony and acquired a land grant. Few women owned land.

New pioneers were pouring into Texas. Jane moved to Brazoria on the Brazos River and opened an inn. William Barret Travis, an attorney from South Carolina, stayed at Jane's inn.

Stephen Austin set off for Mexico, now free from Spain, to ask for the same freedoms for his settlers. The request made the Mexican government angry. Stephen was locked in jail. There he remained for two years, without books or visitors or a trial.

One day, a stranger arrived at Jane's inn. He removed his hat and said, "Lady, I salute you." He had been governor of Tennessee and had lived with the Cherokee Indians in the Oklahoma Territory. His name was Sam Houston.

Finally, Stephen came home. His friends held a supper at Jane's inn. Jane made them leave their guns at the door.

Stephen's love for peace was changed to anger. He told the settlers they must fight for their freedom.

Jane invited friends to come make bullets for the war. One day they practiced firing rifles. Jane was a good hunter. She aimed carefully at the targets. She hit the mark!

Then she served tea.

A message came from William Barret Travis, dated February 1836, calling for help against a larger Mexican army. He was commanding Texas troops at a mission called the Alamo, in San Antonio, Texas, but he was trapped. The battle went on for many days.

William, Davy Crockett, Jim Bowie, and all the defenders of the Alamo died. Jane lost many friends.

Sam Houston, the leader in Texas's War for Independence from Mexico, ordered the settlers to go east toward the United States and safety. Jane and her family joined hundreds of people in the "Runaway Scrape."

Then good news came. Houston and his soldiers defeated the Mexican army at the Battle of San Jacinto, near present-day Houston. Texas was free! Sadly, Jane and the other pioneers returned to find their homes burned.

Some settlers gave up and went back to the United States, but not Jane. She rebuilt her inn. Later, she helped build a school, church, and hotel.

Jane came to Texas as a young woman. The telegraph, the telephone, railroads, and even canning were invented during her lifetime. She saw Texas become a nation and a state. She lived to be eighty-two years old.

Jane's life was a grand adventure. Some call her the Mother of Texas!